Parent Journal

The 5 Seasons of Connection to your Child

Leanne Kabat

The 5 Seasons of Connection To Your Child Parent Journal: Leading Your Family From Chaos to Connection / by Leanne Kabat.

Copyright © 2019 Leanne Kabat

All rights reserved.

No part of this publication may be reproduced, distributed, or transmitted in any form or by any means, including photocopying, recording, or other electronic or mechanical methods, without the prior written permission of the author, except in the case of brief quotations embodied in critical reviews and certain other noncommercial uses permitted by copyright law. For permission requests, email info@leannekabat.com.

Every effort has been made to ensure that the content provided herein is accurate, up-to-date, and helpful to the reader at the time of publishing. This is not an exhaustive treatment of the subject. We encourage anyone to seek help with a professional when the need arises. No liability is assumed. The reader is responsible for the choices, actions and results upon reading this work.

ISBN-13: 978-1-7335410-2-2

Cover design by NewBreed.Design
Interior design by Courtney Michelle & Co. and Leanne Kabat
Published by Leanne Kabat Media
Printed by Gorham Printing, Centralia WA, United States of America

For current content and event info, please visit www.5seasonsofconnection.com

This journal will guide you through the 5 Seasons with your children, becoming a powerful key to unlocking your family's full potential for connection and happiness.

Whatever season you are in right now, know that it can and will get better. With the tools in this journal, deep thinking, and intentional action, you can create the family of your dreams.

This journal is a safe and creative place to explore your feelings, frustrations, struggles and successes as a parent and as a person. When we journal, we externalize the firestorm in our minds, we look at our thoughts objectively, and over time, we see the patterns that keep us in Fall or Winter in our key relationships.

My hope is that you use this journal to its fullest potential to uncover who you are as a parent, what your ideal life with your family looks like, and how to pack enough snacks to get everyone there in one happy, loving, laughing piece!

Our parenting journeys don't look the same, but we do share a core desire to be deeply connected to the most important people in our lives.

I wish you love & sunshine as you take the 5 Seasons framework and make it your own!

Here's to endless Summer days!

xoxo, Leanne

The 5 Seasons of Connection

Winter

Spring

Summer

Fall

Crossroads

What is Winter?

Winter is when you may feel:

- Angry, frustrated, hurt
- Lack of patience
- Uninterested in being around your kids
- Dread when they return home
- Unwilling about to share about your day
- Irritation at all infractions (i.e. leaving dishes out)

In my life, when I am in Winter, I feel...

When my child is in Winter, I notice…

I recognize my family is in Winter when...

What is Spring?

Spring is when you may feel:

- Free from the physical or emotional weight of Winter.
- Happy to enjoy small moments with smiles and laughter.
- The strength to offer forgiveness for past hurts.
- Less friction during conversations and less reactivity.
- Patience and grace, which leads to listening and learning.
- Open to express thoughts, needs, and feelings.

In my life, when I am in Spring, I feel...

When my child is in Spring, I notice…

I recognize my family is in Spring when...

What is Summer?

Summer is when you may feel:

- Happy to be around your kids
- Excited for them to return home
- Open to sharing 'slice of life' stories or childhood tales
- Forgiving of small mistakes, like leaving out the milk
- Emotionally present when socializing with friends
- Confident you can work together on a project/chore

In my life, when I am in Summer, I feel...

When my child is in Summer, I notice…

I recognize my family is in Summer when...

What is Fall?

Fall is when you may feel:

- Caught off guard by something sharp your child says.
- A lack of playful, light feelings in your interactions.
- Physically and emotionally distant from your kids.
- No chit chat, just talking to share necessary info.
- Impatience around their perceived shortcomings.
- A new chill in the air.

In my life, when I am in Fall, I feel...

When my child is in Fall, I notice…

I recognize my family is in Fall when...

What is the Crossroads?

At the Crossroads, you may feel:

- Torn between reacting (Winter emotion) and responding (Summer emotion).
- Anxious about which path to take out of an interaction.
- Emotional, triggered, withdrawn and hesitant, all at once.
- Impatient to get through the interaction or solve the issue.
- Intent to gather all necessary info to make a solid choice.

In my life, when I am at the Crossroads, I feel...

When my child is at the Crossroads, I notice…

I recognize someone in my family is at a Crossroads when...

Winter - Anger

Things that trigger my anger...

Things that calm my anger...

Things that trigger my child's anger...

Other things that can trigger my child's anger...

Hunger	Hormones
Hot	Overwhelm
Cold	Friend Conflict
Stress	Sadness
Illness	Homework
Anxiety	Boredom
Fear	Rejection

Calm Down List

For You or Your Child

- Arrange for quiet time
- Ask for long hug
- Bake muffins
- Bend pipe cleaners into shapes
- Blow a pinwheel or bubbles
- Bounce on yoga ball
- Browse family photo albums
- Brush hair
- Build a maze for marbles
- Build with blocks
- Cartwheel
- Change scenery - go outside
- Chew on chewy jewelry
- Close your eyes
- Color
- Count to 100
- Craft something
- Create paper chain decorations
- Create Shadow Puppets
- Cut snowflakes from folded paper
- Dance
- Do a puzzle
- Doodle
- Draw a picture
- Drink a warm beverage
- Eat
- Exercise
- Go swing
- Hand fidgets
- Have some water
- Hug a stuffed toy
- Hum your favorite song
- I-Spy sensory bottles
- Jump Rope
- Lie under a weighted blanket
- Listen to a rain stick
- Listen to an Audiobook
- Listen to Music
- Listen to nature sounds
- Make a scrapbook page
- Make beaded jewelry
- Make paper basket weaves
- Make silly faces in the mirror
- Paint
- Play an instrument
- Play with pom poms
- Play with your pet
- Playdough or silly putty
- Pop bubble wrap
- Pull on resistance bands
- Put scented lotion on feet
- Read a book
- Read positive affirmations
- Recite your ABC's backwards
- Ride a bike
- Rock in a rocking chair
- Scooter or skateboard
- Scratch and Sniff stickers
- Shake a snow globe
- Sing a song
- Spell out letters in sand tray
- Spin a top
- Squeeze bean bags
- Stretch
- Take a warm bath with oils
- Turn an hourglass
- Use a flashlight in a dark room
- Visualize your happy place
- Watch a lava lamp
- Write in your journal

Spring Planting

Spring is magnificent!

If we think about our family as a garden, and we reflect on how our garden experienced our latest Winter, we can see there is some nurturing and tending needed to help our garden (family) reach its fullest potential.

How will you till the soil, which nutrients will you add, how will you prevent pests and weeds from creeping into your garden so that the seeds you plant now will bloom in your glorious Summer?

Journaling
Self-Care Practices
Boundaries
Well Being Wheel
Apologizing
Forgiveness
Peace Plan
Family Meetings
A.M. / P.M. Routine
Family Meals
Homework
Chores
Screen Time Limits
Books/Music/Play

Spring – Boundaries

A boundary is a line you draw to define where you end and your child begins. When we blur the line, we start to: do things our children can/should do, micromanage their lives, let them run the household with their moods, behaviors or demands, and defer to them to protect the 'friendship.'

If you'd like your child to knock before walking into your room, say 'excuse me' when they need to interject into an adult conversation, or modify other behaviors, let's practice setting a personal boundary here.

Identify a situation when you felt disempowered, stifled, wronged, or resentful

A boundary is a line you draw to define where you end and your child begins. Create a rule that re-establishes your parental power and share it with your child, with clear expectations, desired outcomes, and the natural and appropriate consequence for not respecting the boundary.

Rule

Expectation

Outcome

Consequence

Consistently enforce that rule with your child.
Follow through on consequence when the rule is bent or broken.

Spring- Well Being Wheel

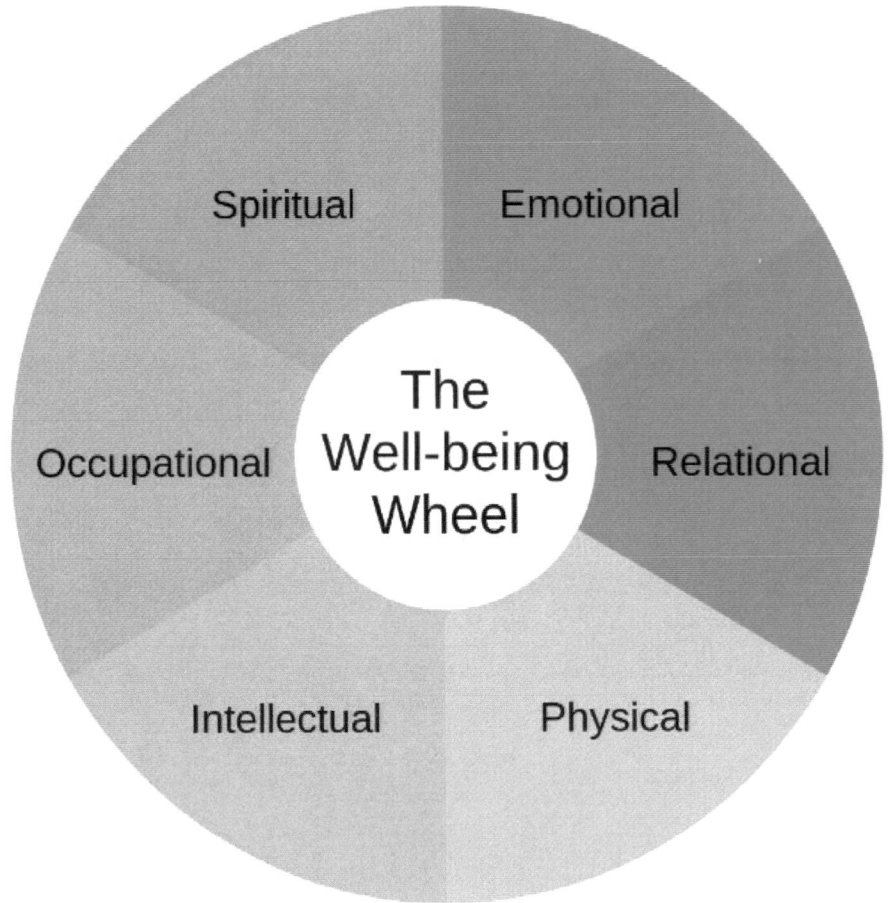

Spiritual – values, meaning, connect to purpose, prayer, meditation, quiet

Emotional – feeling all the feelings, compassion, forgiveness, living love

Relational – strong relationships with kids, partner, parents, good friendships

Physical – good food, hydration, sleep, exercise, stress relief, health checkups

Intellectual – life-long learning, manage time/resources, money, education

Occupational – contributing your talents and skills, problem-solving, career

Spring- Well-Being Check Up

When you examine your well-being, how are you truly doing?
Let's fill out this chart and see what parts of you need a bit of TLC.

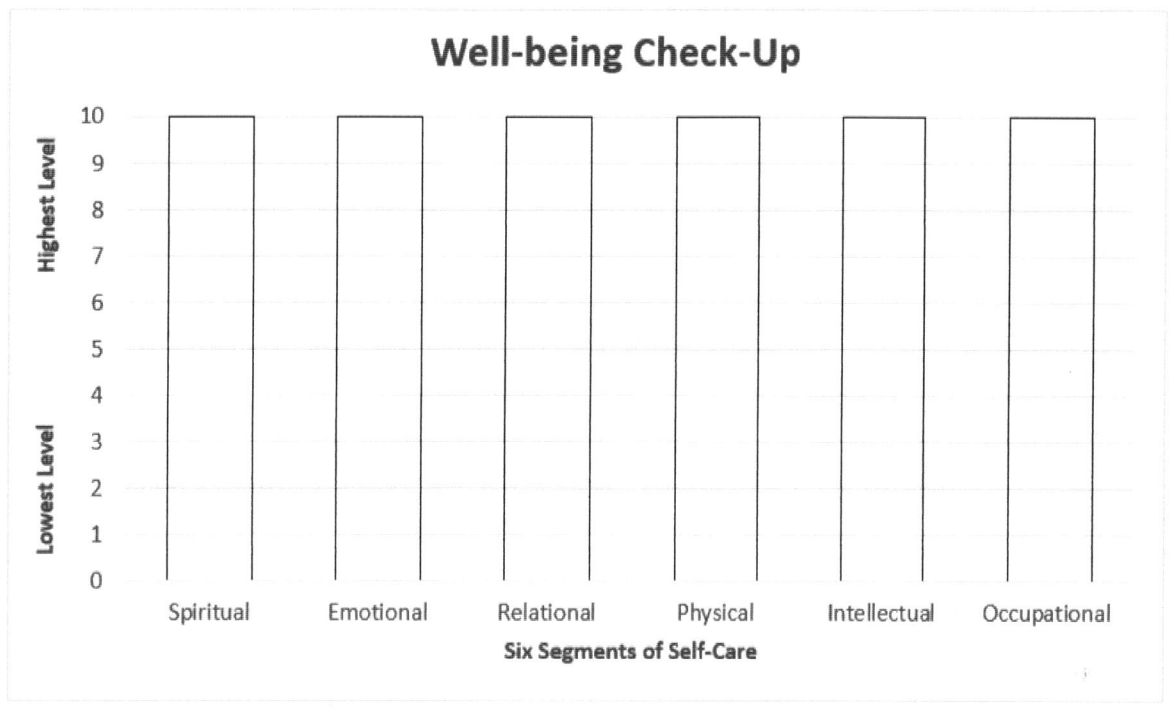

In each category, brainstorm some practices which best support your wellbeing, keeping in mind your interests, lifestyle, budget, resources, and desires.

Spiritual

Emotional

Relational

Physical

Intellectual

Occupational

Spring- Self Care Plan

Now that you've brainstormed some meaningful ways you can tend to your well-being, let's make sure you prioritize them!

Self-Care Section	First Practice I Will Add	Second Practice I Will Add
Spiritual		
Emotional		
Relational		
Physical		
Intellectual		
Occupational		

When you're coming to your relationship nourished, you can better guide your children to create their own meaningful and age-appropriate self-care plans.

Self- Care Section	One practice I can help my child accomplish
Spiritual	
Emotional	
Relational	
Physical	
Intellectual	
Occupational	

this is how we go
Back to Summer

Personal Core Value List

- Ability
- Acceptance
- Accessibility
- Accomplishment
- Accurate
- Achievement
- Adventure
- Ambition
- Appreciation
- Assertive
- Authentic
- Authority
- Balance
- Beauty
- Bold
- Brave
- Calm
- Capable
- Careful
- Challenger
- Charitable
- Cleanliness
- Collaborative
- Community
- Compassionate
- Competent
- Competitive
- Connection
- Contribution
- Cooporation
- Courageous
- Creative
- Curious
- Daring
- Decisive
- Dependable
- Determined
- Diligent
- Dutiful
- Eager
- Education
- Efficient
- Empathetic
- Encouraging
- Energetic
- Entrepreneurial
- Environmental
- Ethical
- Excellence
- Fair
- Faith
- Fame
- Family
- Fearless
- Flexible
- Freedom
- Friendships
- Fun
- Generosity
- Grace
- Gratitude
- Happiness
- Hard working
- Health
- Helpful
- Honesty
- Hopeful
- Humor
- Impact
- Impartial
- Independent
- Innovative
- Inquisitive
- Inspiring
- Integrity
- Intelligent
- Intuitive
- Joy
- Justice
- Kindness
- Knowledge
- Lawful
- Leadership
- Learning
- Listening
- Logical
- Love
- Loyalty
- Meticulous
- Mindful
- Moderate
- Nature
- Openness
- Optimism
- Order
- Organized
- Patient
- Patriotic
- Peace
- Pleasure
- Persistent
- Philanthrophy
- Play
- Positive
- Practical
- Prepared
- Private
- Productive
- Professional
- Realistic
- Reliable
- Resilient
- Resourceful
- Results-oriented
- Religion
- Reputation
- Respect
- Responsible
- Security
- Self-Respect
- Service
- Spirituality
- Simplicity
- Stability
- Status
- Success
- Thoughtful
- Traditional
- Trustworthiness
- Truth
- Understanding
- Unique
- Wealth
- Wisdom
- Wonder

Your Core Values

List your 15-20 core values

Identify your top 10 core values

Choose your top 5-7 core values

Finalize your top 5 personal core values

Family Values

What are the most important things about our family?

What are our strengths?

What words describe us best?

What do you love most about us?

Our Family Values:

Something I want to discuss:

Something I want to suggest:

Something I want help with:

Something I wish was different:

Other things:

This form helps us collect topics for our family meeting this week.
If you need help right away, come find us!

Family Meeting

date _____

Things we are doing well...

Things we could do better...

Upcoming School / Sports / Extra-Curricular Events & Activities

Requested Meals, Snacks

One issue we will work to solve this week...

Fun family activity this week...

Weekly Meal Planner

Week of _____

Monday

Tuesday

Wednesday

Thursday

Friday

Saturday

Sunday

Notes

Special Events

Groceries to purchase

Sample Morning Routine Ideas

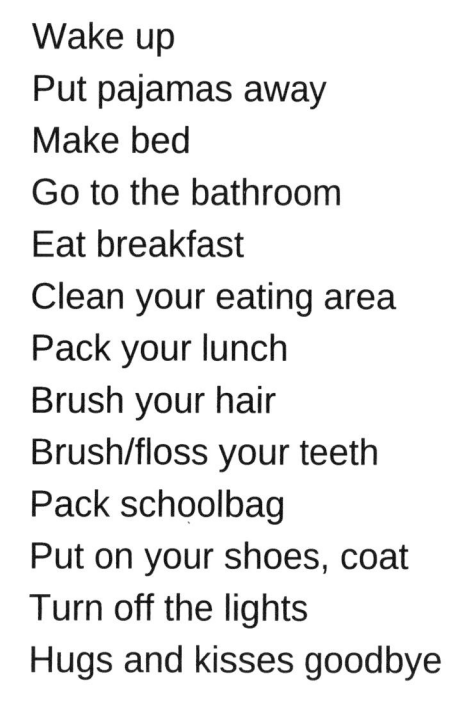

Wake up
Put pajamas away
Make bed
Go to the bathroom
Eat breakfast
Clean your eating area
Pack your lunch
Brush your hair
Brush/floss your teeth
Pack schoolbag
Put on your shoes, coat
Turn off the lights
Hugs and kisses goodbye

Sample Evening Routine Ideas

Empty lunch bag/snack containers
Tidy up after dinner
Complete homework
Complete any chores
Review agenda for tomorrow
Collect everything you need for your day
Clean up toys, art, projects, games
Take bath/shower
Put on pajamas
Brush/floss teeth
Select clothes for tomorrow
Bedtime Story
Evening Gratitude

A.M. Routine for _____

Tasks	Mon	Tues	Wed	Thurs	Fri	Sat	Sun

P.M. Routine for _____

Tasks	Mon	Tues	Wed	Thurs	Fri	Sat	Sun

Chores for Kids

Ages 2-3
- Pick up and put away toys
- Dust tables, shelves
- Collect dirty clothes
- Put clothes away in drawers
- Make bed

Ages 4-5
- *all previous chores
- Set table
- Feed pets
- Match socks
- Pull weeds
- Wipe bathroom counters
- Sweep with cild size broom
- Help load dishwasher

Ages 6-8
- *all previous chores
- Sort laundry
- Collect trash
- Fold clothes
- Help pack school lunch
- Simple snack/meal prep
- Wipe kitchen counters
- Sweep floors
- Vaccum

Ages 9-11
- *all previous chores
- Clean toilets
- Make simple meals
- Clean microwave
- Mop floors
- Wash/dry clothes

Ages 12-14
- *all previous chores
- Clean tub/shower
- Laundry
- Mow lawn
- Watch siblings
- Clean out fridge/freezer
- Make full meals

Ages 15+
- *all previous chores
- Wash car
- Iron clothes
- Trim bushes/edge yard
- Meal plan
- Clean full kitchen
- Buy groceries
- Cook meals

Chore List for _____

Chore	Mon	Tues	Wed	Thurs	Fri	Sat	Sun

Smart Goals

Specific. **M**easurable. **A**chievable. **R**elevant. **T**imely

What are your dream goals?
Brainstorm here!

Specific. **M**easurable. **A**chievable. **R**elevant. **T**imely

GOAL:

List: obstacles, possible solutions, resources.

What obstacles do you foresee preventing you from accomplishing your goal?
What are some solutions or actions that can overcome these obstacles?
Who do you know who could help? What online info or experts can you find?

Obstacles we foresee:

Possible Solutions and Action Items to Overcome Obstacle:

Resources we can access (experts, friends, free/paid, online)

Specific. Measurable. Achievable. Relevant. Timely

Goal:

Action Items & Tasks

List at least five action items or tasks to help you achieve your goal.
Assign target and completion dates.

	Action or Task	Target Date	Completed Date
1.			
2.			
3.			
4.			
5.			
6.			

How will you reward your family once you've accomplished your goal?

Weekly Planner

Your time. The most precious resource you have.

One the first planner page, create your IDEAL week, making sure to prioritize and schedule all the things that matter (ie exercise, meditation, date nights, game night with your kids, self-care).

On the second planner page, track and log your ACTUAL week.

Yikes! I bet you see two very different calendars!
It's okay, we are taking charge of our time.

Are there time-sucks you can cut out?
Things you can automate? Eliminate? Delegate?
Meaningful things you want to add in?
Social activities or hobbies you have neglected?
Playful activities with your kids?

When you identify your priorities and purposefully align your calendar with those priorities, you win and your kids win!

My Ideal Week

	Sunday	Monday	Tuesday	Wednesday	Thursday	Friday	Saturday
6am							
7am							
8am							
9am							
10am							
11am							
12pm							
1pm							
2pm							
3pm							
4pm							
5pm							
6pm							
7pm							
8pm							
9pm							
10pm							

My Priorities

When I was completing *My Ideal Week*, I realized I want these things to be prioritized in my life AND scheduled in my calendar:

My Actual Week

	Sunday	Monday	Tuesday	Wednesday	Thursday	Friday	Saturday
6am							
7am							
8am							
9am							
10am							
11am							
12pm							
1pm							
2pm							
3pm							
4pm							
5pm							
6pm							
7pm							
8pm							
9pm							
10pm							

Respecting My Time

Now that I see how I spend my time, what will I change so my calendar aligns with my priorities, my core values, and my family values?

Things to CONSOLIDATE

Things to DELEGATE

Things to ELIMINATE

Our Plans

One secret to sprinkling Summer throughout your year is to plan activities that bring your family to Summer!
Use this calendar to track and plan some upcoming fun!

January

February

March

April

May

June

Our Plans

July

August

September

October

November

December

Temperament

1. Activity Level: how active is your child most of the time?

2. Distractibility: how easily do outside influences distract your child?

3. Intensity: how much intensity does your child have in her responses?

4. Regularity: does your child vary in her eating or sleeping patterns?

5. Sensory Threshold: how sensitive is your child to physical sensations?

6. Approach/Withdrawal: how does your child respond to strangers?

7. Adaptability: how easily does your child adapt to changes in his day?

8. Persistence: how long will your child work to solve something hard?

9. Mood: is your child a glass half empty or half full kind of person?

Complete the chart on the next page to identify your children's temperaments so you can work with their natural tendencies and move towards Summer.

Temperament Chart

	Child _____	Child _____	Child _____
Activity			
Distractibility			
Intensity			
Regularity			
Sensory			
Approach			
Adaptability			
Persistence			
Mood			

	Child _____	Child _____	Child _____
Activity			
Distractibility			
Intensity			
Regularity			
Sensory			
Approach			
Adaptability			
Persistence			
Mood			

The 5 Love Languages

According to Dr. Gary Chapman, creator of The 5 Love Languages, our children will have one primary and one secondary love language. They are:

Quality Time	Words of Affirmation	Gifts
Physical Touch	Acts of Service	

One language will rise up as being the more dominant love language for our children when we observe them with these questions in mind:

1. How does my child express love to me?
2. How does my child express love to others (siblings, teachers)?
3. What does my child ask for the most?
4. What does my child complain about the most?

Your child may show you her preferences early, or later - either way is fine! However, it doesn't help the mama who is stressing out that she has to deliver on all 5 strategies all the time! Not to worry, there is a very unscientific and experimental exercise you can do in the comfort of your life to help identify which few rise to the top, and which few fall to the bottom of the list.

It's a game I play with my kids called: **Would You Rather?**

The main idea is to offer two different scenarios and see which one your child selects, but it's not a one and done! If your child picks one way of connecting over another, it doesn't mean that one time determines a winner.

If you go for ice cream and your child picks raspberry sorbet – it doesn't mean she wants that flavor only and always. Just like any experiment, you should run it multiple days in multiple ways to test and retest. You can do it casually, or for my beautiful super-performers who want to track it a little more intentionally, I have set up a table based on a sports tournament bracket.

You can use whatever questions that fit your life to test what method of connection your child prefers. I provide some examples below but there are limitless ways to do this so don't feel constrained to do it this way at all!

Example Questions for a Younger Child

1. I see you aren't feeling well, I'm sorry you aren't up to going to the park! Would you rather work on a puzzle with me (quality time) or would you like me to clean up your toys (acts of service) while you rest?

2. When I return back from my work trip, would you rather me bring you a small present (gift) or a story that write for you about what a sweet girl you are and how much I missed you (words of affirmation)?

3. Would you rather I gave you a foot rub (physical touch) or read you a story (quality time)?

Example Questions for a Tween Child:

1. For winning your soccer tournament, would you rather I bought you a new ball (gift) or go out for a celebration lunch (quality time)?

2. We have so much energy today! Would you rather wrestle with me on the carpet (physical touch) or I clean the trampoline so you can jump (acts of service)?

3. When we go to daddy's work picnic tomorrow, would you rather I share your story of winning the spelling bee with the other families we meet (words of affirmation) or would you rather we join the scavenger hunt (quality time)?

Example Questions for a Teen Child:

1. I'm home early tonight. Would you rather we go play tennis (quality time) or I upgrade the memory on your computer (acts of service)?

2. If I notice you feeling discouraged after your school exam and I wanted to cheer you up, would you rather I give you a big hug (physical touch) or tell you lots of positive things I know to be true about you (words of affirmation)?

3. For your 16th birthday, would you rather I give you $300 (gift) or take you on a weekend getaway (quality time)?

Would You Rather?

Round #	Love language 1	vs	Love Language 2	My child preferred:
Round 1	Gifts	vs	Physical Touch	
Round 2	Words of Affirm.	vs	Quality Time	
Round 3	Physical Touch	vs	Words of Affirm.	
Round 4	Acts of Service	vs	Gifts	
Round 5	Words of Affirm.	vs	Acts of Service	
Round 6	Quality Time	vs	Physical Touch	
Round 7	Acts of Service	vs	Quality Time	
Round 8	Gifts	vs	Words of Affirm.	
Round 9	Quality Time	vs	Gifts	
Round 10	Physical Touch	vs	Acts of Service	
Round 11	Physical Touch	vs	Gifts	
Round 12	Quality Time	vs	Words of Affirm.	
Round 13	Words of Affirm.	vs	Physical Touch	
Round 14	Gifts	vs	Acts of Service	
Round 15	Acts of Service	vs	Words of Affirm.	
Round 16	Physical Touch	vs	Quality Time	
Round 17	Quality Time	vs	Acts of Service	
Round 18	Words of Affirm.	vs	Gifts	
Round 19	Gifts	vs	Quality Time	
Round 20	Acts of Service	vs	Physical Touch	

_____'s Love Language is _____

_____'s Love Language is _____

_____'s Love Language is _____

_____'s Love Language is _____

Notes

I'm so very grateful for...

(Write on each ray)

Your Journal

Here is where the rubber hits the road. It's time to get honest with yourself about your hopes, dreams, fears, anxieties, struggles and successes on your personal and parenting journey.

You can follow the prompts or freestyle write, but most importantly, give yourself the time and space to explore, discover and feel *all the feelings*. Uncover your hurts. Validate your experiences. It's okay, you will need to go into some deep Winter memories or confront some big fears to get to your Summer. Give yourself the support you need. Heal your heart. Dream new dreams. This is by you, for you. Make it your own.

I believe in you!

xoxo Leanne

I want to write, but more than that, I want to bring out all kinds of things that lie buried deep in my heart.
~ Anne Frank, The Diary of Anne Frank

How do I feel as a parent right now?

I sustain myself with the love of family.
~ Maya Angelou

What do I need to bring myself to Summer?

Family is not an important thing, it's everything.
~ Michael J. Fox, Actor

What is going right in my family and in my life?

Family means no one gets left behind or forgotten.
~ David Ogden Stiers, Actor

What is something itchy that I need to deal with before it pushes me to Winter?

What can you do to promote world peace?
Go home and love your family.
~ Mother Teresa

What am I prioritizing in my family and in my life right now?

Other things may change us, but we start and end with family.
~ Anthony Brandt, Author

What makes me come alive?

The family is one of nature's masterpieces.
~ George Santayana, Spanish Philosopher

What old wound in my soul can I heal so I can be the parent I dream of being?

*Each day of our lives we make deposits in
the memory banks of our children.
~ Charles R. Swindoll, Pastor*

What am I totally rocking in my parenting right now?

Family is the most important thing in the world.
~ Princess Diana

What would I try if I knew I couldn't stumble, fall or fail?

*While we try to teach our children all about life,
our children teach us what life is all about.
~ Angela Schwindt, Homeschooling Mom*

I'd love to learn…

A mother's love for her child is like nothing else in the world. It knows no law, no pity, it dares all things and crushes down remorselessly all that stands in its path.
~ Agatha Christie, Author

I can nurture and nourish myself today by…

Rejoice with your family in the beautiful land of life.
~ Albert Einstein

When did I overcome something that first felt impossible?

*Unconditional love is loving your kids for who they are,
not for what they do… it isn't something you will achieve every minute of
every day. But it is the thought we must hold in our hearts every day.*
~ Stephanie Marston, Author and Speaker

What would I love to do with my family right now?

Families are the compass that guides us. They are the inspiration to reach great heights, and our comfort when we occasionally falter.
~ Brad Henry, Lawyer and Politician

How do I get through a hard day?

Love your family. Be for them who you want for you.
  ~ Unknown

What makes me the happiest?

*My family is my life, and everything else comes second
as far as what's important to me.*
~ Michael Imperioli, Actor

What do I miss most about my pre-mama days?

*You go through life wondering what is it all about,
but at the end of the day it's all about family.
~ Rod Stewart, Musician*

Today, I am so grateful for…

Children are people, and they should have to reach to learn about things, to understand things, just as adults have to reach if they want to grow in mental stature. Life is composed of lights and shadows, and we would be untruthful, insincere, and saccharine if we tried to pretend there were no shadows. Most things are good, and they are the strongest things; but there are evil things too, and you are not doing a child a favor by trying to shield him from reality. The important thing is to teach a child that good can always triumph over evil.
~ Walt Disney

What worries me most about my kids is …

Family: Where life begins and love never ends.
~ Unknown

The family rituals I love most are…

*It's not our job to toughen our children up to face a cruel and heartless world.
It's our job to raise children who will make the world a little less cruel and
heartless.*
~ L.R. Knost, Author

As a parent, I am most surprised by…

*When you become a parent, you reveal a part of you that
you hadn't met before. Be kind to her, she's new at this.
~ Unknown*

What is my ideal morning routine?

*If you want children to keep their feet on the ground,
put some responsibility on their shoulders.
~ Abigail Van Buren, aka Dear Abby columnist*

I can support my child through a hard day by…

*Don't worry that children never listen to you;
worry that they are always watching you.
~ Robert Fulghum, Author*

I am like and unlike my parents in these ways…

Many believe that parenting is about controlling children's behavior and training them to act like adults. I believe that parenting is about controlling my own behavior and acting like an adult myself. Children learn what they live and live what they learn.
~ L.R. Knost, Author

My top hot button issue right now is...

*The uncertainty of parenting can bring up feelings in us
that range from frustration to terror.*
~ Brene Brown, Author

My family would work better together right now if...

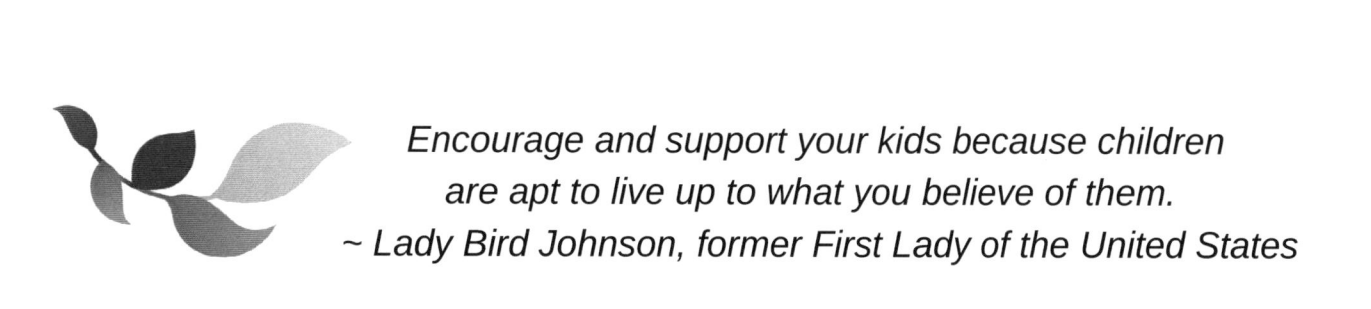

*Encourage and support your kids because children
are apt to live up to what you believe of them.*
~ Lady Bird Johnson, former First Lady of the United States

If we could travel anywhere as a family, we would go to…

The way we talk to our children becomes their inner voice.
~ Peggy O'Mara, Blogger

What are the ways I nurture my creative side?

What it's like to be a parent: It's one of the hardest things you'll ever do but in exchange it teaches you the meaning of unconditional love.
~ Nicholas Sparks, Author

What are my dreams for my child's future?

*24/7. Once you sign on to be a mother,
that's the only shift they offer.
~ Jodi Picoult, Author*

What self-care practices do I want to teach my child?

My father gave me the greatest gift anyone could give another person, he believed in me.
~ Jim Valvano, Basketball Coach and Broadcaster

If I received $500, what would I do with it?

Have patience with all things. But, first of all with yourself.
~ Saint Francis de Sales

What friendships do I want to reinvigorate?

*Before I got married, I had six theories about raising children;
now, I have six children and no theories.
~ John Wilmot, 2nd Earl of Rochester (1647-1680)*

My favorite way to spend the day is…

*There are only two lasting bequests we can hope to give our children.
One of these is roots, the other, wings.*
~ Hodding Carter, Author

I couldn't imagine living without…

*All of us have moments in our lives that test our courage.
Taking children into a house with white carpet is one of them.
~ Erma Bombeck, Author*

When I'm in pain (emotional/physical/spiritual), the kindest thing I can do for myself is…

*Never cut a tree down in the wintertime. Never make a negative decision in the low time. Never make your most important decisions when you are in your worst moods. Wait. Be patient. The storm will pass.
The spring will come.
~ Robert H. Schuller, Author and Pastor*

How would it feel to love myself unconditionally?

*There's a feeling sometimes in motherhood that you're alone in
what you're going through, and none of us are alone.
We're all going through the same thing.*
~ Nia Vardalos, Actor

How easy is it for me to forgive those who have caused me pain?

*In giving birth to our babies, we may find that we
give birth to new possibilities within ourselves.*
~ Myla and Jon Kabat-Zinn, Authors

What do I love about my life today?

The reality is that most of us communicate the same way we grew up. That communication style becomes our normal way of dealing with issues, our blueprint for communication. It's what we know and pass on to our own children. We either become our childhood or we make a conscious choice to change it.
~ Kristen Crockett, Author

My biggest mistakes have taught me…

I have seen many storms in my life. Most storms have caught me by surprise, so I had to learn very quickly to look further and understand that I am not capable of controlling the weather, to exercise the art of patience and to respect the fury of nature.
~ Paulo Coehho, Author

I feel most energized when…

I feel most energized when…

*Making the decision to have a child is momentous.
It is to decide forever to have your heart
go walking around outside your body.
~ Elizabeth Stone, Author*

The most fun I've ever had with my kids was . . .

Affirming words from moms and dads are like light switches. Speak a word of affirmation at the right moment in a child's life and it's like lighting up a whole roomful of possibilities.
~ Gary Smalley, Family Therapist

What's one thing I could do to go deeper into Summer today?

I think that the best thing we can do for our children is to allow them to do things for themselves, allow them to be strong, allow them to experience life on their own terms… let them believe more in themselves.
~ C. JoyBell C., Author

I feel most stressed when…

Sometimes, kids want you to hurt the way they hurt. ~ Mitch Albom, Author

When I was in Winter with my child, I learned…

Being a mother is learning about strengths you didn't know you had and dealing with fears you didn't know existed.
~ Linda Wooten, Author

'hat did I do today to bring me closer to my dream (life, family, trip, career, relationship, etc.)

If you can control your behavior when everything around you is out of control, you can model for your children a valuable lesson in patience and understanding...and snatch an opportunity to shape character.
~ Jane Clayson Johnson, Author

How do I deal with emotional blizzards?

*Instead of communicating, "I love you, let me make life easy for you,"
I decided my message needed to be something more along these lines: "I
love you. I believe in you. I know what you're capable of.
So I'm going to make you work."
~ Kay Wills Wyma, Author*

If I could learn one thing to help me, it would be…

No one is ever quite ready; everyone is always caught off guard. Parenthood chooses you. And you open your eyes, look at what you've got, say "Oh, my gosh," and recognize that of all the balls there ever were, this is the one you should not drop. It's not a question of choice.
~ Marisa de los Santos, Author

When things are hard, I want to remember…

Being a parent is dirty and scary and beautiful and hard and miraculous and exhausting and thankless and joyful and frustrating all at once.
It's everything.
~ Jill Smokler, Author

I can help my child grow in confidence by…

Motherhood has completely changed me. It's just about the most completely humbling experience I've ever had. I think it puts you in your place because it really forces you to address the issues that you claim to believe in and if you can't stand up to those principles when you're raising a child, forget it.
~ Diane Keaton, Actor

The one habit I want to create but haven't yet is...

To us, family means putting your arms around each other and being there.
~ Barbara Bush, Former First Lady of the United States

The compliment I hear most often about my kids is...

Your children will become what you are; so be what you want them to be.
~ David Bly, Former Teacher and Politician

An adventure I would love to have with my child is...

No matter how far we come, our parents are always in us.
~ Brad Meltzer, Author

I am inspired by….

My most important title is "mom-in-chief". My daughters are still the heart of my heart and the center of my world.
~ Michelle Obama,
[my favorite] Former First Lady of the United States

My anger…

*In every conceivable manner,
the family is link to our past, bridge to our future.*
~ *Alex Haley, Author*

The dominant emotion in my life right now is...

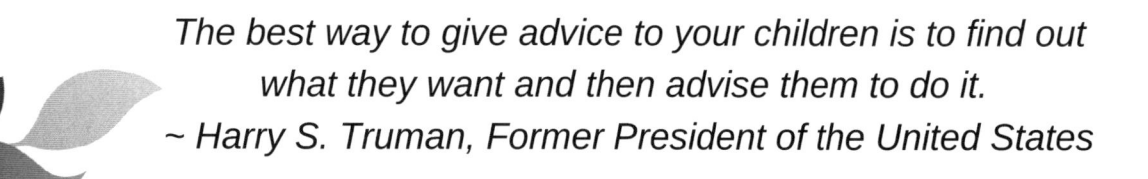

The best way to give advice to your children is to find out what they want and then advise them to do it.
~ Harry S. Truman, Former President of the United States

The most disappointed I've ever been as a parent. . .

*I loved you enough to accept you for what you are,
not what I wanted you to be.*
~ Erma Bombeck, Author

Today, I am grateful for…

The most important jewels that will ever be wrapped around your neck are the arms of your children. Good job Mamas.
~ Pink, Singer

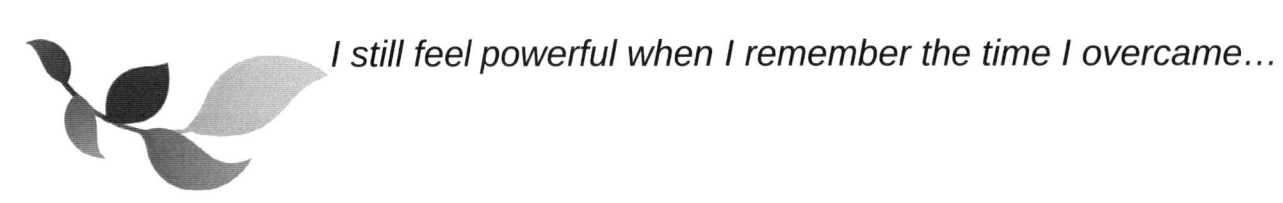

I still feel powerful when I remember the time I overcame…

Motherhood has taught me the meaning of living in the moment and being at peace. Children don't think about yesterday, and they don't think about tomorrow. They just exist in the moment.
~ Jessalyn Gilsig, Actor

I can see Fall coming when…

We cannot give our children what we don't have.
~ Brene Brown, Author

The Spring Cleaning strategies I will use in my life are...

He didn't realize that love as powerful as your mother's for you leaves its own mark.
~ J.K. Rowling, Harry Potter and the Sorcerer's Stone

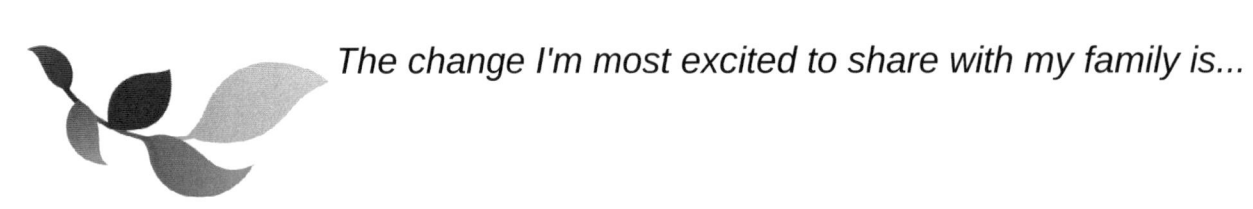

The change I'm most excited to share with my family is...

Parenthood...It's about guiding the next generation, and forgiving the last.
~ Peter Krause, Actor

My time matters. From now on, I'm going to say no to...

I used to believe my father about everything but then I had children myself and now I see how much stuff you make up just to keep yourself from going crazy.
~ Brian Andreas, Artist

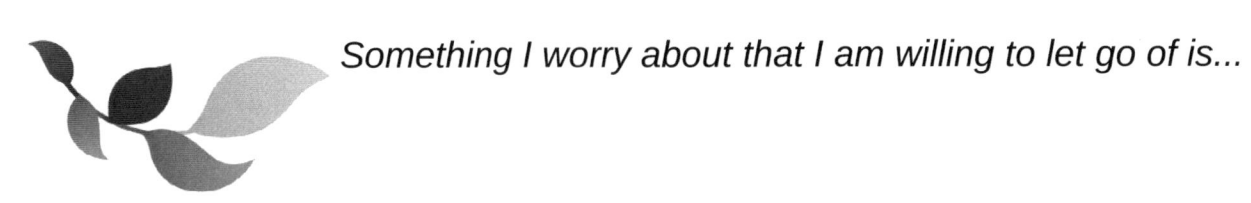

Something I worry about that I am willing to let go of is...

By loving them for more than their abilities we show our children that they are much more than the sum of their accomplishments.
~ Eileen Kennedy-Moore, Author

One long-neglected thing I need to make a priority is...

There is no single effort more radical in its potential for saving the world than a transformation of the way we raise our children.
~ Marianne Williamson, Author

Some movies I want to share with my child include…

Through the blur, I wondered if I was alone or if other parents felt the same way I did - that everything involving our children was painful in some way. The emotions, whether they were joy, sorrow, love or pride, were so deep and sharp that in the end they left you raw, exposed and yes, in pain. The human heart was not designed to beat outside the human body and yet, each child represented just that - a parent's heart bared, beating forever outside its chest.
~ Debra Ginsberg, Author

The last time my child melted my heart was...

What lingers from the parent's individual past, unresolved or incomplete, often becomes part of her or his irrational parenting.
~ Virginia Satir, Author and Therapist

Something I want to say 'YES' to more often is... .

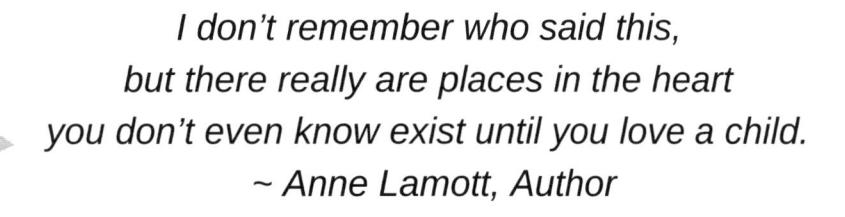

*I don't remember who said this,
but there really are places in the heart
you don't even know exist until you love a child.*
~ Anne Lamott, Author

As a mom, I know for sure…

In the end, that's what being a parent is all about—those precious moments with our children that fill us with pride and excitement for their future, the chances we have to set an example or offer a piece of advice, the opportunities to just be there and show them that we love them.
~ Barack Obama,
[my favorite] Former President of the United States